© **Copyright 2024 - All rights reserved.**

The content contained within this book may not be reproduced, duplicated or transmitted without direct written permission from the author or the publisher.

Under no circumstances will any blame or legal responsibility be held against the publisher, or author, for any damages, reparation, or monetary loss due to the information contained within this book, either directly or indirectly.

Legal Notice:

This book is copyright protected. It is only for personal use. You cannot amend, distribute, sell, use, quote or paraphrase any part, or the content within this book, without the consent of the author or publisher.

Disclaimer Notice:

Please note the information contained within this document is for educational and entertainment purposes only. All effort has been executed to present accurate, up to date, reliable, complete information. No warranties of any kind are declared or implied. Readers acknowledge that the author is not engaged in the rendering of legal, financial, medical or professional advice. The content within this book has been derived from various sources. Please consult a licensed professional before attempting any techniques outlined in this book.

By reading this document, the reader agrees that under no circumstances is the author responsible for any losses, direct or indirect, that are incurred as a result of the use of the information contained within this document, including, but not limited to, errors, omissions, or inaccuracies.

Table of Contents

                                                                                              Page

Introduction -- 1

Story 1: The First Taraweeh in Riyadh ---------------------------- 2

Story 2: Lanterns in Cairo -- 5

Story 3: Breaking Fast in Dakar ---------------------------------- 8

Story 4: Ramadan in My Classroom ------------------------------ 11

Story 5: Moonlit Prayers in Jakarta ------------------------------ 14

Story 6: A Drummer's Dawn in Istanbul -------------------------- 17

Story 7: Iftar Delights in Dhaka ---------------------------------- 20

Closing Reflections -- 23

Introduction

Ramadan represents a month of introspection, generosity, and joyous celebration for Muslims worldwide. It provides an opportunity to bond with family, extend aid to those less fortunate, and deepen our connection with Allah via fasting and prayer.

However, have you ever considered how varied Ramadan traditions can be depending on geographical location?

In this enlightening book, we will introduce you from every corner of the world who celebrate Ramadan in their unique ways. From the lantern-illuminated streets of Cairo to the colorfully extravagant iftar feasts in Dhaka - from the tranquil mosques of Jakarta to the bustling community meals in Dakar - each narrative will start you on an extraordinary journey brimming with love, delight, and wisdom.

So ignite your imagination and prepare yourself to traverse the globe through the perspective of diverse children reveling in this enchanting month. Let's commence our adventure!

Story 1: "The First Taraweeh in Riyadh"

Location: Riyadh, Saudi Arabia

In Riyadh, Saudi Arabia, Ahmed assists his father in preparing dates freshly harvested from their family's farm. These soft, golden fruits are sweet and sticky – an ideal choice to break a fast as once done by Prophet Muhammad (Peace be upon him).

A steaming pot of kabsa graces the table - this spiced rice dish is studded with tender lamb chunks and caramelized onions. The air fills with aromatic spices like saffron, cinnamon, and cardamom that reflect the heartwarming richness of Arabian hospitality. Bowls filled with cool cucumber yogurt salad offer a refreshing balance to the meal.

For Ahmed though, luqaimat steals the show - these golden fried dumplings drizzled with date syrup are his favourite part of the meal. He eagerly shares them with his siblings embodying Ramadan's spirit of generosity.

3

Color the golden luqaimat dumplings and the kabsa rice dish the plate below. Write their names in the blanks below!

4

Story 2: "Lanterns in Cairo"

Location: Cairo, Egypt

In the bustling heart of Cairo, young Youssef and his little sister Layla eagerly anticipate the call to iftar. The streets radiate with vibrant fanoos (lanterns), while the enticing aroma of freshly baked bread and roasted meats fills the air.

As Youssef's family congregates with their neighbors, an array of mouth-watering dishes begin to populate the table. There's a simmering pot of lentil soup - thick, hearty, subtly infused with cumin and garlic.

A towering platter of koshari stands proudly amongst other dishes - it's layers of rice, lentils, pasta crowned with crispy fried onions and tangy tomato sauce.

This cherished dish epitomizes Egypt's communal spirit during Ramadan - a tradition where everyone contributes something for the meal. The feast concludes on a sweet note with syrup-drenched basbousa – a semolina cake bathed in rosewater syrup – accompanied by refreshing hibiscus tea that leaves everyone contented and prepared for prayer.

6

Color the fanoos (lantern) and the delicious layers of rice, lentils, and pasta. Can you label both?

7

Story 3: "Breaking Fast in Dakar"

Location: Dakar, Senegal

Mamadou and his family love the community spirit of Ramadan. As the sun begins to set, Mamadou assists his mother in preparing ndambe - a hearty bean stew simmering with tomatoes, onions, and garlic. This dish, a staple in Senegalese iftars, reflects the country's emphasis on warmth and simplicity in breaking the fast. The rich aroma fills their home, promising comfort after a day of fasting.

When the call to prayer sounds, the family breaks their fast with bowls of creamy millet porridge sweetened with honey and milk. The velvety texture of the porridge beautifully contrasts with the sweet delightfulness of thiakry, a dessert of couscous mixed with yogurt, sugar, and raisins. This combination of dishes not only nourishes the body but celebrates the Senegalese values of sharing and hospitality during Ramadan.

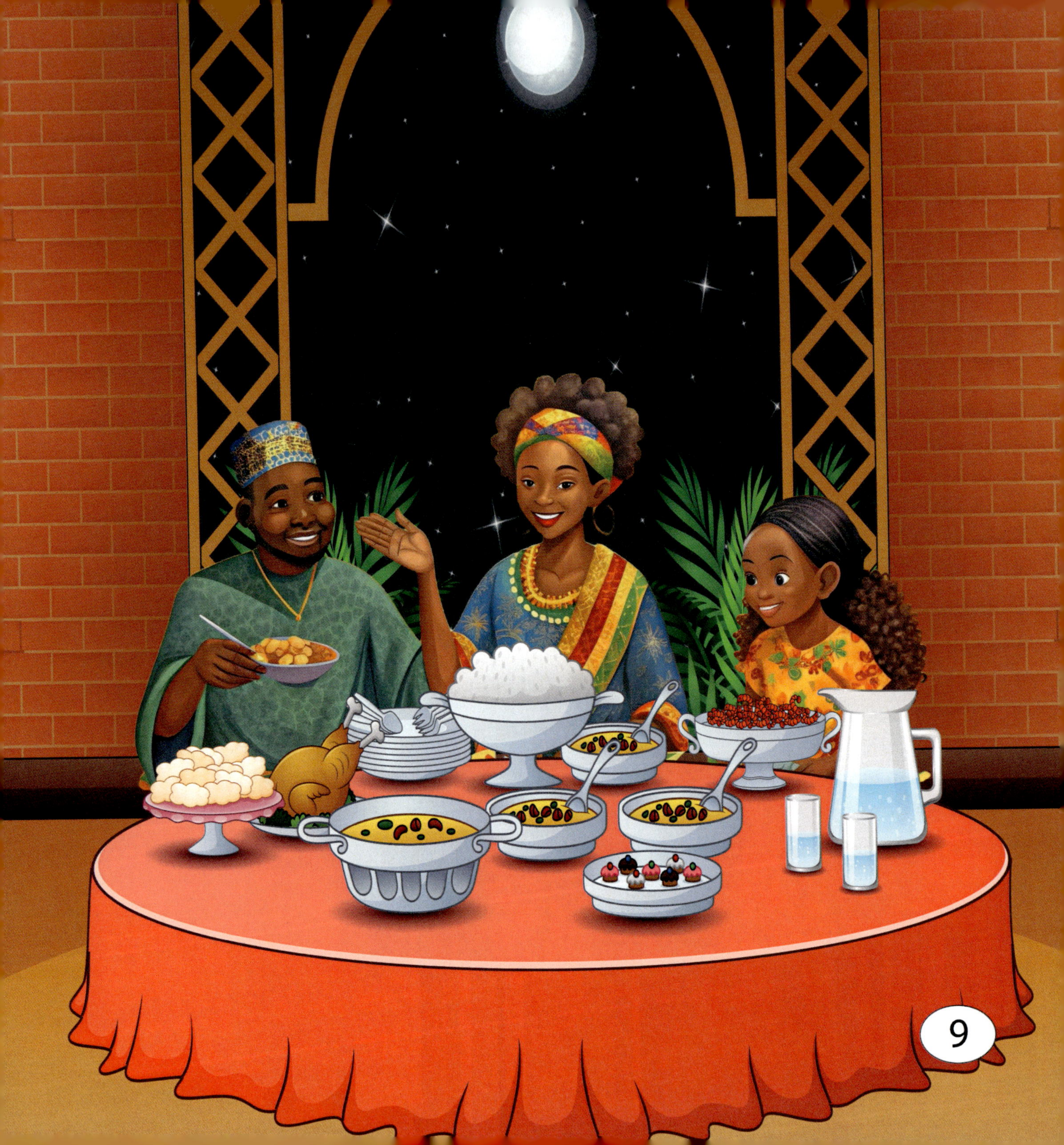

Color the creamy millet porridge and the sweet thiakry dessert. Can you name them both below?

Story 4: "Ramadan in My Classroom"

Location: Chicago, USA

Sophia, an enthusiastic Muslim-American student, eagerly shares her experience of Ramadan with her classmates. She brings dates to school along with a beautiful Ramadan lantern and an informative poster about her family's traditions.

When some friends inquire why she skips lunch, Sophia enlightens them about the significance of fasting and introspection during this holy month.

Later on, Sophia warmly invites her friends over for iftar at her home. They start their meal with succulent Medjool dates paired with tall glasses of refreshing milk - a customary way to break the fast that harks back to Prophet Muhammad's (peace be upon him) time.

The table groans under platters brimming with flavorful kebabs, buttery rice dishes, and spiced vegetables - it's an inviting showcase of the diverse culinary heritage found within American Muslim cultures.

For dessert? Sophias mom serves up delicious baklava – it's crispy layers filled with honeyed nuts elicit delighted smiles from their guests.

12

Color the plate of kebabs, buttery rice, and baklava on Sophia's table. Write their names below to share with your friends.

13

Story 5: "Moonlit Prayers in Jakarta"

Location: Jakarta, Indonesia

Rina resides in Jakarta, a city where the onset of Ramadan is marked by a vibrant parade known as dugderan. She unites with her family at the mosque on the inaugural night of Tarawih prayers. The mosque is beautifully decorated, and the melodious recitation of the Quran fills the air.

For iftar, Rina and her family enjoy kolak, a dessert made with bananas, sweet potatoes, and tapioca pearls swimming in rich coconut milk sweetened with palm sugar. This warm, creamy delight holds pride of place as a family favorite, embodying not just comforting flavors from home and symbolizing unity and shared joy during Ramadan. Its caramel-like richness is savored by families across Indonesia as a way to break their fast.

15

Color the creamy kolak dessert made with bananas and sweet potatoes. Write its name below!

16

Story 6: "A Drummer's Dawn in Istanbul"

Location: Istanbul, Turkey

Ali is roused from sleep by the rhythmic beat of the drummer, summoning people to suhoor. He gathers with his family for a light meal of olives, cheese, and pide bread - fresh from the oven and speckled with sesame seeds. This soft, chewy bread is even more delightful when coupled with creamy yogurt and honey drizzle. This ritual underscore Turkey's focus on beginning the fasting day with straightforward yet nutritious foods that bring families closer.

At iftar time, they reconvene to share warm lentil soup infused with lemon zest and mint leaves, followed by crispy börek filled generously with spinach and feta cheese. Dessert is lokma - small dough balls deep-fried till golden brown then soaked in sweet syrup until they melt upon contact with your tongue.

These delicacies, deeply rooted in Ottoman traditions spanning centuries, underscore Turkey's rich culinary heritage during Ramadan.

18

Color the round pide bread with sesame seeds and the golden lokma dessert. Can you write their names below?

19

Story 7: "Iftar Delights in Dhaka"

Location: Dhaka, Bangladesh

Sara lives in Dhaka, where the city transforms during Ramadan. She relishes her strolls through the lively lanes of Old Dhaka, where food stalls tempt passersby with their offerings of crispy piyaju (lentil fritters), delicious beguni (fried eggplant slices), and sugary jelapi.

Each bite into the golden-brown piyaju results in an enticing crackle, unveiling it's soft and spiced core, meanwhile, the jelapi - twisted into shapes reminiscent of radiant orange jewels - drip generously with sugar syrup that lovingly adheres to Sara's fingers. These snacks are part of Bangladesh's rich iftar tradition, where families and neighbors share plates of homemade and street-bought delights to break their fast together.

Her grandmother masterfully prepares a hearty bowlful of chola, spiced chickpeas cooked with tamarind, green chilies, and fragrant mustard oil. This dish, passed down through generations, reflects the bold and tangy flavors of Bangladeshi cuisine. The whole family gathers to break their fast, savoring every flavorful dish before the evening prayer.

21

Color the crispy piyaju, golden jalebi, and fried beguni. Don't forget to name them all!

22

Closing Reflections:

The uniqueness of each country's Ramadan traditions shines through, in their flavorful dishes and in their distinctive ways of celebrating with family and community. Whether it's the sweet jalebi of Dhaka, the hearty kabsa of Riyadh, or the creamy kolak of Jakarta, these foods hold special meanings and are deeply tied to each culture's history and heritage.

Yet, amidst these differences lies a unifying thread that binds Muslims everywhere during Ramadan - fasting for Allah, cultivating gratitude, and fortifying faith. The shared purpose of devotion and unity is what makes Ramadan so special. This sacred period sees Muslims worldwide uniting in worship, embodying generosity and love while valuing the myriad expressions of these virtues.

That encapsulates the beauty inherent in being a Muslim—honoring shared faith whilst cherishing rich generational as well as cultural traditions that render every Ramadan experience distinctively beautiful."

Author Note

Dear reader,

Thank you so much for reading this book. I hope this book has brought warmth and inspiration to your family's moments of reflection and learning. Your feedback is a precious gift that helps authors nurture young hearts and minds in their Islamic education. Please share your valuable thoughts through a customer review. Your insights will guide us in spreading messages of Islam and love to children everywhere.

Thank you for being a part of our shared mission!

Enhance your child's Ramadan experience with the Ramadan Journal for Kids—a heartfelt guide to reflection, creativity, and spiritual growth.

Available to order now to inspire a meaningful journey this blessed season.

Keep the Ramadan spirit alive daily with the "Ramadan Journal for Kids: A Ramadan Gift for Kids." Packed with 30 days of inspiring duas, fun fasting and Suhoor trackers, and creative art spaces, this journal helps our young learners capture every special moment of this blessed month. Start an unforgettable Ramadan journey for your little one —get the journal now!

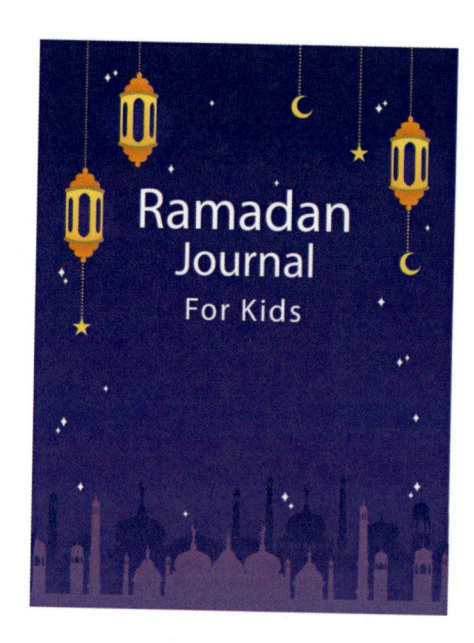

Discover the magic of Ramadan as celebrated by children across the globe in **"Ramadan Around the World : Ramadan Stories for Kids."** This heartwarming collection of stories invites young readers to explore the vibrant traditions, delicious tfoods, and shared values of the holy month, from the lantern-lit streets of Cairo to the joyful community feasts in Dakar.

Through these captivating tales, your child will:

- **Journey to diverse countries** and experience Ramadan through the eyes of children ust like them.
- **Learn Islamic values** such as gratitude, generosity, and unity woven into every story.
- **Celebrate cultural diversity** while strengthening their connection to the shared beauty of Islam.
- **Engage with interactive activities** designed to spark creativity and deepen understanding.

Whether it's savoring the sweet luqaimat of Riyadh, coloring the glowing fanoos of Cairo, or reflecting on the lessons of Ramadan in a Chicago classroom, this book offers a unique blend of education and inspiration.

Written especially for Muslim children raised in multicultural settings, **"Ramadan Around the World: Ramadan Stories for Kids "** bridges tradition and modernity, helping kids embrace their faith while appreciating the rich tapestry of global Muslim communities.

Perfect for bedtime reading, classroom discussions, or Ramadan gifting, this book is a treasure for every family's library.